A
LIST

T0162546

ALSO BY ERÍN MOURE

Poetry (or as indicated)

Empire, York Street (Anansi, 1979)

Wanted Alive (Anansi, 1983)

Domestic Fuel (Anansi, 1985)

WSW (West South West) (Véhicule, 1989)

Sheepish Beauty, Civilian Love (Véhicule, 1992)

Search Procedures (Anansi, 1996)

A Frame of the Book (or *The Frame of a Book*) (Anansi, 1999)

Pillage Laud (Moveable Type, 1999, BookThug, 2011)

O Cidadán (Anansi, 2002)

Little Theatres (Anansi, 2005)

O Cadoiro (Anansi, 2007)

My Beloved Wager (NeWest Press, 2009, essays)

Expeditions of a Chimæra (with Oana Avasilichioaei, BookThug, 2009)

O Resplandor (Anansi, 2010)

The Unmemntioable (Anansi, 2012)

Insecession (with Chus Pato's *Secession* in Moure translation, BookThug, 2014, biopoetics)

Kapusta (Anansi, 2015)

Planetary Noise: Selected Poetry of Erín Moure, ed. Shannon Maguire (Wesleyan University Press, 2017)

Sitting Shiva on Minto Avenue, by Toots (New Star Books, 2017, memoir)

Selected Translations

Installations, by Nicole Brossard (with Robert Majzels, Muses' Company, 2000)

Sheep's Vigil by a Fervent Person, by Fernando Pessoa (Anansi, 2001, 2004)

Museum of Bone and Water, by Nicole Brossard (with Robert Majzels, Anansi, 2003)

Notebook of Roses and Civilization, by Nicole Brossard (with Robert Majzels, Coach House, 2007)

Charenton, by Chus Pato (Shearsman, 2007)

quase flanders, quase extramadura, by Andrés Ajens (La Mano Izquierda, 2008)

m-Talá, by Chus Pato (Shearsman, 2009)

Hordes of Writing, by Chus Pato (Shearsman, 2011)

Just Like Her, by Louise Dupré (Wolsak & Wynn, 2011)

Galician Songs, by Rosalía de Castro (Small Stations, 2013)

White Piano, by Nicole Brossard (with Robert Majzels, Coach House, 2013)

My Dinosaur, by François Turcot (BookThug, 2016)

Flesh of Leviathan, by Chus Pato (Omnidawn, 2016)

New Leaves, by Rosalía de Castro (Small Stations, 2016)

Paraguayan Sea, by Wilson Bueno (Nightboat, 2017)

FURIOUS
ERÍN MOURE

LIST

First published in 1988 by House of Anansi Press Ltd.
This edition published in Canada in 2018 and the USA in 2018 by
House of Anansi Press Inc.
www.houseofanansi.com

22 21 20 19 18   1 2 3 4 5

Library and Archives Canada Cataloguing in Publication

Mouré, Erin, 1955-, author
Furious / Erin Mouré.

Poems.
Previously published: Toronto : Anansi, 1988.
Issued in print and electronic formats.
ISBN 978-1-4870-0428-6 (softcover).—ISBN 978-1-4870-0429-3
(PDF)

I. Title.

PS8576.O96F87 2018   C811'.54   C2018-900056-2
                            C2018-903319-3

Library of Congress Control Number: 2017964350

Series design: Brian Morgan
Cover illustration: Vida Simon
Typesetting: Sara Loos

*We acknowledge for their financial support of our publishing program
the Canada Council for the Arts, the Ontario Arts Council, and the Government of Canada.*

Printed and bound in Canada

INTRODUCTION
by Sonnet L'Abbé

It's the way people use language makes me furious. The ones who reject the colloquial & common culture. The ones who laud on the other hand the common & denigrate the intellect, as if we are not thinking. The ones who play between the two, as if culture is a strong wind blowing in the path of *honour*. It takes us nowhere & makes me furious, is all.

THESE RESTLESS, PASSIONATE lines appear near the end of Erín Moure's landmark poetry collection, *Furious*. They are part of a section called "The Acts," wherein Moure lays out a manifesto of sorts, a statement of what she means poetry to do. Behind their fury is a deep faith that language can be used more consciously, more ethically, to take us *somewhere*. That somewhere, for Moure, is a kinder world, a place of respectful and joyous interrelation.

All poets probably believe that bringing poetry into existence makes the world a better place. But the question of how poetry does that, how *language* does that, and what exactly we might mean by "better," is one that many poets leave unexamined. Only a few ask about language's structures, and these structures' relation to the body, perception, and action. And among those few, it is the rare poet who can synthesize these relations into an effective, *affective* new approach, expanding our sense of what poetry can do, and changing our notion of what poetry even is.

Erín Moure is such a poet. Moure's work has "altered the conditions of possibility for poets of several generations," writes Shannon Maguire, in her introduction to Moure's selected poems. "Moure is one of those rare poets that seems to have created her own school out of disparate, desperate, and seemingly unrelated strands of other writing, other histories, and other lines of thinking, becoming something entirely her own," says Rob McLennan. *Furious* is Moure's fourth book. It won the 1988 Governor General's Award for Poetry, which, Maguire reminds us, was "Canada's most prestigious national poetry award at that time, an equivalent of an American Pulitzer Prize." *Furious* is the collection where we see Moure leap, from an earlier phase of writing lyric explorations of working-class and lesbian consciousness, into her uniquely radical, language-deconstructing, possibility-opening poetics.

But *Furious* is not important only because we see in it a style evolution of a major Canadian poet establishing some of the core themes of her oeuvre (like multi-voicedness, queer desire, daughterhood, and cabbages). *Furious* is, as Rachel Zolf has put it, a "feminist poetry classic," because the fury that Moure voices, and the stylistic leap she takes in faith that the way we use language matters, did not flower in isolation.

Pauline Butling asked Moure why her poetics shifted so dramatically with the publication of *Furious*. Moure said: "I think a real catalyst or turning point for me was the Women and Words conference of 1983. It opened up my thinking about women and language." The bilingual conference, described as "a watershed event, ... represent[ing] the culmination of more than a decade of feminist activism on many fronts," attracted over a thousand women to Vancouver and included such speakers as Nicole Brossard, Maria Campbell, Betsy Warland, Makeda Silvera, Phyllis Webb, Claire Harris, and Louise Cotnoir. Cotnoir told the assembled group: "Language is biased and (women) are the ones that suffer this bias ... we are fighting against the social order that has defined us by its language." Women were searching for a new language to express their realities and their desires.

Women and Words encouraged many Anglophone Canadian women to embrace new French feminist theory that asserted the possibility of an *écriture féminine*. Shortly after the conference, Moure moved to Montréal, where she met like-minded women with whom she could discuss the ideas of Julia Kristeva, Luce Irigaray, Hélène Cixous, and Jacques Derrida. One of these women was Gail Scott, who helped Moure (who spoke only "railway French" at the time) access French writing and questioned many of Moure's attitudes. "With *Furious*," says Moure, "Gail and the space she opened up for me were very important. ... She used to ask me why I acted as if thinking and writing were separate. ... I started writing down what I was thinking when I was writing some of the poems, how I was trying to think out the poem." *Furious* comes out of these vibrant conversations, both public and personal, that pushed Moure increasingly toward seeing "writing a poem" and "theorizing about language" as indistinguishable from one another.

Furious is organized into two movements, poems and "The Acts." The first movement, "Pure Reason," is divided into three subsections, "Pure Reason," "Visible Affection," and "Furious." In the first, we are invited to consider the shared embodiedness of vegetables, animals and humans, and how the thinking of "our damn heads" perpetuates ideas of human exceptionalism. The rational men who are the moral agents of Kantian philosophy are presented as colleagues whose "mouths are opening above their male ties, spilling molecules of air across the room & their jobs are filling up with their bodies, their jobs are the shape of their bodies."

In the second section, lesbian love is made visible, and we see the power of writing lesbian desire to disrupt the orders of man-made language. "At last," we can hear the "howl" of two women whose love has been shut "between parentheses." Moure writes, "I touch her with my mouth," and it sounds like the act of speaking a poem to a lover. Moure experiments at using words to name the world women desire, to "[walk] away, from the word *cock*, & *ravishment* / To name what our own tongues will call *something*."

In the third and eponymous section, Moure's poems attempt to speak with the "mouth, hurt" by colonial and sexist language. Her voice fights through the brain-habit of conventional, commodifying English, striving to speak of physical knowing "until none of us is angry."

The second movement, "The Acts," are like the poet's notes to herself. We can imagine her writing them as she composed the poems. It is as though Moure heard an entire generation of women asking for a new feminist language, and went back to her workshop to invent it. "It isn't that to change the weight and force of English will *necessarily* make women's speaking possible. But to move the force in any language, create a slippage, *even for a moment...*"

Moure's work is sometimes described as difficult. Some of the poems of *Furious* can feel disjointed, as though the speaker interrupts herself. Perhaps she jumps from one thought to another without clueing us in to the three or four connections she made between them. Perhaps she falls silent, mid-sentence, because the English language ceases to be adequate to express the knowing or being at hand. Perhaps she is pausing to eat a sandwich or kiss. Perhaps she is tearing syntax down to build new relationships between parts of speech, to utter "The Motion before the Name." If you can't always follow, don't worry. Moure assures us: "I want the overall sound to be one of making sense, but I don't want the inside of the poem to make sense of anything. // People who are making sense are just making me laugh, is all."

In November 2017, *Lemonhound 3.0* republished the first six "Acts," calling *Furious* an "essential collection." Indeed, the book is an essential act of literary feminism, language theory, and poetry. You could say we are living in the "not-yet," the "to-come," the *somewhere,* of *Furious.* The questions that Moure furiously asked then, about how we might advance feminist goals by deconstructing language, critiquing Western ideas of rationality, and insisting on human and non-human bodies as the ground of cognition, are the larger questions that helped make today's understandings of relationality, gender identity, and inclusive language possible. Thirty years after its original publication, the core fury of *Furious*—that how some people use language takes us nowhere—and the core faith—that committed writing can take us toward a kinder world—remain as necessary as ever.

SONNET L'ABBÉ, Ph.D., is the author of *A Strange Relief* and *Killarnoe,* and was the 2014 guest editor of Best Canadian Poetry. Her chapbook, *Anima Canadensis,* was published by Junction Books in 2016 and won the 2017 bpNichol Chapbook Award. In her next collection, *Sonnet's Shakespeare,* L'Abbé "writes over" all 154 of Shakespeare's sonnets. L'Abbé is a professor of Creative Writing and English at Vancouver Island University.

FURIOUS

ACK NOW LEDGE MENT SS

(Immeasurable) thanks to Gail Scott, whose fiction, voice, and thinking helped seed the light that is in this book.

Andrew Wreggitt and Ken Mouré each read this book in process. James Polk of Anansi edited, and sent my mind in new directions at the last minute. Libby Scheier wouldn't let me give up.

The poem "Whose" owes a line to John Newlove's poem "And The Dead Rose Up From The Water" (*Lies* 1972).

The poem "Irish Eyes" owes a line to Robinson Jeffers' poem "Hurt Hawks" (*Cawdor and Other Poems* 1928). It also contains lyric snippets from the song "When Irish Eyes Are Smiling" by Chauncey Olcott and George Graff, Jr. (1912).

The poem "Gorgeous" contains brief (slightly misquoted) references to D.H. Lawrence's poem "Snake" (1921) and to the first poem in Rainer Maria Rilke's *Duino Elegies* (1923).

The cover drawing is by Vida Simon and was commissioned especially for this edition. Thank you, Vida!

"To inhabit freely the civic house of memory..."

Some of these poems first appeared in:

Island
Event
Northern Light
Montréal Now
Dandelion
The Dinosaur Review
Prism international
HERizons
Brick
The New Quarterly
The Capilano Review
Canadian Literature
Poetry Montréal
Matrix
Descant
Fireweed
Poetry Canada Review
Bending Moment
Deep Down: The New Sensual Writing by Women, ed. Laura Chester
blue buffalo

CONTENTS

The footnotes refer to The Acts. pp. 81–97.

1. PURE REASON

Pure Reason

Visible Affection

Culture has been chattering and chattering but to no purpose. When a sentence becomes distinct, it makes no more sense or connection. Wherefore, the watcher says again "Unintelligible", nods his head, and smiles gloomily. He puts a few coins on the table, grabs a cap, gropes his way down the broken stairs, mumbles good-morning to some rat-ridden super sitting in an old plastic chair under the stairs, and passes out.

Kathy Acker
Great Expectations

1. PURE REASON

Pure Reason

Whose

In whose garden I am sleeping
In whose garden I am sleeping perfectly,
the round cabbages with their blue-green leaves,
slug-dust on the outer border, a few ragged zinnias,
perfectly sleeping,
wearing the pea-trellis shadow over my pyjama,
listening to the carrot rooted in the earth,
its pointed microphone listening for water,
orange & hidden,
flawless
I am sleeping
It is true I am only sleeping
it is true that my fingers are uncurled & bothering no one,
the beets with their heads downward,
the row by row, the drug of topsoil,
lettuce & zucchini, their leaves & waiting,
my knees pulled up & feet splayed outward,
in whose garden,
refusing a few years to abandon my despair.

Goodbye to Beef

The irrational deafness of our heads, that's
all.
Where our elegant coiffure comes from,
our own fingers, hey: squirrel-
hunting in the Rocky Mountains under the smell of spruce
forest I said I never would forget
& haven't.
Damn it.
Where our research will get us,
home free, sliding fast
past the hard throw from second baseman.
Looking for just one more homer.

We are listening to too much music, & our tastes
are lousy.

The squirrel my brother shot down with the .22 so the dog could play.
The dog just sniffed the dead fur
& looked up the tree again, eye
cocked for the squirrel.
It is always in our damn heads.

Or my head.

Or anyone's.

When we got together, what we talked of,
the moose my uncle shot & cut up into frozen pieces,
& sent it down, in 1964, on the Greyhound.

What I forgot to say, was:
When we saw that box of moose hefted out of the bus bay in
the din of yelling navvies,
we knew it was goodbye to beef
till springtime.

& I haven't talked to my aunt since.

I go deaf thinking of it. Or anything.

Pure Reason: Having

Having the most to lose.
Having a steadie gaze, &
most of all, a haircut.
Having sent everything to the laundry, even
the unlaunderable.
Having a *photocopy* of a page of *writing* taken
from a *magazine*.
I am in the car of my father with a mug of sweet coffee
outside Red Deer Alberta in the white of winter
wearing the coat I've had twelve years
& not liking the coffee, either.
Between Edmonton & Calgary, the roads are closed by snow.
Drifts on the highway & hard wind
moving who knows where.

Having forgotten my destination
Having been capable of shyness
Having been shy
Having kissed my family on their nearest shoulders

What the highway is, pointing without slope or vision.
Its re-constructed dream
empty, finally
except for the curves & overpasses, the centre median.
To be, always, capable.
To move the jaw in & out, as if biting
hard.
To be reckless.

To be on the road. This early.
Wherever we are going.
Wherever my parents drive.

Seated ahead of me. Their heads faced away.
Sculptures of apples.
The cold visible, white

Snow Door

Trying to remember, as if
The music, as if, as if

The music fell into my boots & I couldn't
wear them, couldn' t feel.

The scent of orange behind the room's door...that note...
Physical space,   physical
                                          space

Space between the window & its frame where the wind enters,
chilling the chairs. Dead flies between the panes, winter flies that
come to life when they warm up, but go stupid from the freezing, &
can't remember flight exactly, not exact enough, they topple on their
backs & spin & buzz. Having forgotten everything except that they
used to fly, why can't they do it now. Too stupid to know why they
can't do it now.

Us, too,
who don't know we've been frozen, or if we have, &
if we know, don't ask questions.

I know I know.

My colleagues' mouths are opening above their male ties, spilling
molecules of air across the room, & I am this sad when I see it
spilling, no one else watches & I can't tell them, they are *serious,* &
their jobs are filling up with their bodies, their jobs are the shape of
their bodies, I see their lives

fluttering, behind.

The woman I once knew
who reached her right hand into the glow & gripped the spoon,
flaming,
the physical reproduction of anguish
denial of physics
defiance   revenge

Snow door snow door snow door snow

Affectively, as if
The blizzard was over, we cur holes in the snowbanks,
our razor hearts burnished, our shovels raised up like sheet metal
As sentences, to make us   feel

Pure Reason: Science

The day the animals came on the radio, fed-up, the electrodes in their hands
beaming, small tubes leading into their brains where chemicals enter,
& the bubbling light from that, the experiment
of science,
the washed fur on their faces & in their voice

The quick brown fox jumped over the lazy dog is a comparison we reject,
they say. Leading to the obvious:

Maple _sugar_ comes from maple _trees_.

Animals in the laboratories, their small chests
cut open where the wires are, the tough protective hairs & sensory
reception, high-pitched hearing,
on the radio, sonant, re/
plying to science that is hurting them for diet soft drinks,
they say,
how the light of our poisoned colons shines
its fine beam into the cells of animal brains
As if you could dream like we dream & be cured, the animals say,
pushing back the announcer,
showing off into the microphone the cut scars
of our diet fantasy
inside which their babies are waiting with our defects
to be born

Eventually I came to miss the mountains, the man said
hands knotted in front of his jacket
in the Faculty bar of an English university
in Montréal where the heat stifles
No, I don't miss them, the mountains, the woman
said, perhaps
you depended upon them, &
I became them, she said, they're here with me now
in this hot room
inside my body head resting, otherwise, she said
this is just another metaphor
for sexual difference, she said, crossing out
line after line &
George Vancouver the healer stepping into the trees,
his boat fluttered with flags, or
the place Mr. Fraser came out into the delta & was frightened
The woman putting her coat on in the heat

Oh little lamb, who made thee, she said & stood up,
hugging the woman she came with, in her painfulness & quiet,
their arms close & hands open, the fear they'd been through
unspeakable, from the West to the West,
& their affection,
laughing

Irish Eyes

The failure of the new.
Its stories built on the mountain painted beyond the window,
Mexico City fallen in, 7.6 on the Richter scale.
B flat, otherwise known. Lionel's trumpet
in the hazy dark of the boîte à jazz, wiping his mouth
& lifting his eyes up. Getting ready to scale it
with plastic wrap, pinions, *the broken wing jags*
from the clotted shoulder, whatever.

The slight headache lift of the head, where the tongue should be,
above the fault-line, the blue lichened trees, scraped rock,
& we are instead, seeing, tourism.
The red river valley.
The motels in Ft. Lauderdale.
No one here remembers John McCormack so she stands up,
a drunk woman in a doorway singing: *Irish Eyes.*
For & against the house payments.
The getting-together of any two humans, & their children,
human children.
She sang & fell over, the words ran out of the side of her head,
heavily, on the way home.

Where are we going anywhere.
Where are we going the inside of this car.

When Irish eyes are smiling, she said,
sure it's like a morn in spring
In the lilt of Irish laughter, she said,
you can hear the angels sing

& if so, why has the new failed.
Blunt acceleration up the side of the mountain.
(*Terriffic tea*, wrote Maura's mother in the guest book, at the foot of it)

Pure Reason: Femininity

The day the women came on the radio, fed-up, electrodes in their purses
beaming, small rubes leading into their brains where doctors enter,
the bubbling light from that, neuronic balance, the de/pression
of their inner houses,

washed skin on their faces & in their voice

She belongs to a certain class of women whose
profession is to promote lust is a comparison we reject,
they say to the judge. Leading to the
obvious:

Deathful *thinking* comes from deathful *minds*.

Women in the earth are not so powerless, their soft chests
torn open where the pin-ups were, the tough protective skin & sensory
reception, the high-pitched hearing,
on the radio, their subjective loudness, sonant, re/
plying to justice that divides them into classes,
they say,
how the light of the soft cock under the black robe shines
its fine beam into the cells of women's brains
As if you could dream like we dream & be cured, the women say on the radio,
pushing back the announcer,
showing off into the microphone the cut scars
of obstetrics out of which their babies have been pulled out, held
by doctors, newly *born*

Fifteen Years

I am in a daydream of my uncle,
his shirt out at his daughter's wedding,
white scoop of the shirt-tail bobbing
on the dance floor.
When I think of it.
When I think of my cousin, otherwise,
shooting the BB gun up the exhaust pipe of his motorcycle,
behind the garage.
It is the softness of a puppy we have brought home from the farm,
& set on the grass to fall over crying,
sleeping in a boot next to the heart-tick of the alarm.

I am wondering how we live at all
unable to replace these images.
The green space beside my parents' house in summer
where we lay down on our stomachs to keep cool.
My uncle's shirt-tail beneath his suit jacket, dancing.
The flag of that shirt-tail.
I tell you.
His daughter married for fifteen years.

Thirteen Years

I am in a daydream of my uncle,
his shirt out at his daughter's wedding,
white scoop of the shirt-tail bobbing
on the dance floor & him in it, no,
his drunk friend pawing me, it was *his* shirt dangling,
I forgot this,
my youngest cousin in his dress pants downing straight whisky,
& me too, tying tin cans to his sister's car.
The sour taste of it. Drink this, he said.

I am wondering how we live at all
or if we do.
The puppy we grew up with came from the same uncle's farm.
His shirt-tail beneath his suit jacket, dancing.
The friend of the family touching my new chest.
They told me not to say so.
I'll drive you to the motel, he said, his breath close.
No. Be nice to him, they said, & waved me off from the table.
I was so scared.
Everyone had been drinking. Including me. Thirteen years old.
Who the hell did my cousin marry.
I tell you.

A History of Vietnam & Central America as Seen in the
Paintings of Leon Golub, *Musée des beaux arts, Montréal, 1985*

Several sections of this photograph are not visible.
Several sections have been repaired.
Several pieces of this canvas have been torn out
or covered over.
Several sections have been smeared.
If you turn around the photograph the result
is not the backs of heads.
The result of one painting sawn in three
is three paintings.
Several sections of this paragraph have been repaired.
Several sections have been forged with outside influence.
The woman holding the man's cock in the painting was also painted
by the man.
If the eye sees & the mouth describes.
If several sections of this photograph are not visible.
If the corn in the field winnowed new
teeth smiling
Several sanctions of this painting have been recently
restored
There is no speaking torn out & lifted says the president
There is no section of this painting you do not see

Several sections of this photograph have been torn out.
Several sections have been replaced.
Several parts of this poem are encoded to prevent theft
of language.
Several parts of this poem are encoded by theft,
to prevent language.
The mercenaries hold silver guns, they are throwing
the artist's body into the trunk of an American car.
Several pictures have not been taken.
Several times I have not stopped listing over.
The photograph gets smaller in the fingers.
When it is over we stand up & walk out, our breath fast,
uncreasing our knees

23

The grey heart touched by the lips turns red.
My red sweater, the colour of that touch.
Trees bowed trees bowed trees
Thinking of the poem <u>Snow Door</u>.
Bronwen writes me of her back yard in Kingston
& I am thinking of the grass growing there by the fence &
Bron inside the house at 11am, sleeping, blankets tossed over her.

A small photograph of the inside of the head shows
an ordinary cranium.
An empty vessel makes the most noise
the student tells me,
explaining his silence & my virtual
noise.

The connections between poetic syllables
have finally broken down.
We pushed on them so long our arms were hurting.

A glass earring.
Bron's boyfriend in the driveway, looking at a white canoe.

None of us has solved sexual longing.
At a café table, a woman sings the rock hero of New Jersey
more slowly than the record.
Already she is days behind.
We are only recognized from our passports
for five minutes at any border.

I'm on fire. she sings

Cure

I am thinking of the cross-grain slices
they cut out of cows, in their centre being,
their fleshy fullness.

Sometimes I am only the piece of liver in me, its cell walls
permeable & unbutchered
Its huge slice grows in me, instead of children
I am growing this organ
When I raise it in my arms to show you
it flops, a wet flag, awkward

Red & blind.
I am the blind immensity, of my liver, its
immense blindness.
I cry when I see the livers of so many cows folded with their water
into the plastic cups of meat counters.

Outside, rain creeps its breath
into the leaves, drenching their pores.

Those cows moving in the field, freely & captive, their memory
timed
down to the kill floor, so many seconds for the head blow,
so many to lance away the skin.

If the liver were soft enough to hold up
in my mouth without hurting,
I could call my memory out of it

I could taste what is in me that won't ever be
clean.

Palm Sunday

I to whom friends come before their trips,
I have so many suitcases

Palm Sunday: The life line, the heart line, the
head line, & the line of fate

Footsteps into the courtyard & back out,
carrying an old-fashioned television, too heavy,
full of rubes

Boxes of flowers grow on my table in the kitchen
under the narrow light, living the edge of
danger, *so little light*

1 out of 3 women, assaulted sexually, in their lives.

Listening to the World Series in 1968, our eyes
dry, Sirhan Sirhan jailed,
Melissa in the back of Grade 8 geography, an earphone
under her hair,
cheering for the Detroit Tigers.

All of us
remember
some of
some thing

or we wouldn't be here.

We scrub & scrub our rooftops, trying to please.
Please be clean. Please clean me.

Please please me, sang the top rock group with the
same haircut, we traded gum cards of their faces
on the front lawn in the hot summer green of

1965.

In the picture, my brother sits on the front step, small,
wearing the green nylon jacket passed down from the rest of us,
smiling concretely.

1 out of 3 women assaulted.
The locks changed & the windows impregnable.

The word "impregnable".
What are we saying.
(Impossible) to theorize about the real.

With a Small Comb

With a small comb my hair is looking better & better
With an earring of silver my voice
shines in my ear,

with a map of Uruguay I am going to a friend of the butcher,
to ask what part of the cow it comes from
& how I will eat it when it arrives

Because I have ordered it,
I have taken out my pen & ordered it with a jar of whisky
concealed in a small sock in a suitcase

in the suitcase I threw behind the house yesterday
where it filled up with water
in this morning's rain

Now I want to go somewhere I cannot
Now I want to go somewhere I can only wet my clothes in it
Now I want to go somewhere

yes, somewhere, because
my hair is looking better,
it is looking better, thank you, it is looking so good.

Visible Affection

Rolling Motion

Your face in my neck &
arms dwelling upward face
in my soft leg open
lifted upward airborne soft
face into under into rolling
over every upward motion
rolling open over your
Face in my neck again over
turning risen touch billows
my mouth open enter
dwelling upward face
in your soft leg open
lifted upward airborne soft
face into under into motion
over every upward open
rolling open over your
Face in my neck again
& arms

Aspen

Woman whose arms are the bones of the poem,
full of indispensible marrow

Her mouth is a lone cry behind
an aspen, the weeds grown tangled, cow parsnip, brown canes of
raspberry, sunlight,
I touch her with my mouth

& our two cries flutter,
impossible havoc, heat, haven, have-not of the body,
our tensions in its arms & folded openings in its centre,
where we touch the cry
without knowing its sense
finally
deep inside the marrow
Hushed in each other for a moment, the leaves still

before we separate
& it begins again, each cry
behind its aspen, each aspen
clattering its leaves in sunlight, dropping silver onto the floor

Rose

In the house between parentheses, the howl.
O lady of the blessed flowers,
our lady of suicide, our lady of the top floor, lady leaning
over the rooftop, hair over her third eye,
open, finally.
At last, at last.

The wind between the towers is nothing but the wind, nothing but the.
Our displacement is huge & wild & does not see the fish
in their houses under the pavement,
their hair combed.
I too have combed my hair.
I too have asked Christ to be my mother, with his hair I want to touch
& soft apron I buried my eyes in, all those years.
I too have worn my famous airplane on my shoulders, its
two wheels spinning.
I too am female am not truthful am not am not

To covet.
At least, this: covet.
The small torn mark in the centre of my skull's plate, where I landed
upside down off my bicycle on Motorcycle Hill.
Do you remember.
When I am telling you do you ever remember.
Do you remember your hair & the light rose blouse you wore
when we were walking over the railway, & I kissed you
& the cars honked, & we were two women without stopping...

Speaking of Which

The silver paper from the bottles, torn & rolled up, are
our diamonds, or
thrown up into the scarce air: stars.
By these stars you know us, don't you.

By these official stars.

Inside our lungs small hands are blessing each globe
of air, small lips are kissing us,
red, unlit, hot oxygen torn out & pushed
into the bloodstream,

we move our elbows on & off the crowded table, we are women with
this & *this* dream, we have eaten in *these* places, we slept with
men or boys at the age of, at the age of, too young,
wanting to see what it was, that body,

then finally,
not caring for it,
not dreaming of it either except as a sign, like the outside of a house
when the walls are burning, a sign
like hallways, or diamonds, that body

We wanted to see it knowing how little it would mean,
how little of our past it would bring back to us,
how little…

The small clear globes of oxygen, our lungs & the rivulet
of anger they touch & keep warm,
its long passage of heat & fury under the skin, to all extremity,

because this fury is our hardest core, because the bar is full of women's
talk & whispers, by these signs you shall know us,

the bright oxygen, the air inside us who stared
then walked away, from the word *cock*, & *ravishment*
To name what our own tongues will call *something*,

our arms close to each other, so close, the ashtray full up
with diamonds, our diamonds, our firstborn stars

The Blind

The seven kinds of beauty, inside the heart, fuel in the hallway
of the blood. Our tainted light brown skin taut pulled over the nerve-tissue,
thriving, the city of bones & light. Is is is us.

Children on their tricycles, playing
loud games in the dust behind the apartment, the boy in sunglasses,
takes the bicycle away from the girl. What he can do, &
she cannot, is is is
, with difficulty, learned.

Learned, with difficulty.

As if, beauty too, is difficult, is the stubborn flavour of the blood licked
from the cut hand, hammer-stroking nails into the wall, the lathe, the
80 year old plaster, hand-made, beautiful, choking on the dust,
we dream with dust in our hair of a day on the front step in the light
where we are, oh,   just sitting

Nothing magnificent. Having just passed the razor mark of thirty,
to enter a middle age. The back aches
more readily. We suppose we are are are what? —
oh, financially more viable, perhaps, we've learned
too, to make the most of a moment, even if it is not ours,
or if it is
technological, that old bug-bear,
the jet stream cutting the blue heat of the sky

which is also, I tell you, beautiful.
What is beautiful lasts such a short time, except in the nerve-tissue where it
burns alive once we have seen it. Or felt, because some of us are blind, &
to us, there is so much more that is beautiful,
because what things *say* or *feel like*
is now also

the Visible,

nervous a bit

Meeting

Meeting implies purpose. The Vietnamese boy sweeping the floor
also makes good
coffee
& owns
this restaurant where the woman pats the yellow curled dog on the terrasse
& a boy does Tai Chi in the doorway the ache
in my back is the same ache I feel
for your mouth on those open places their tenderness the
tenderness of blind birds soft asleep
in their shells their feathers pin-small combed flat with
mucous hair & bird thoughts of the dome-light shining
thru the egg the earth the way light shines
thru the fingers, opalescent, the way a woman sitting
forward rubs her soft lidded centre on the chair's cloth
the texture of that
the restaurant where I sit today, good coffee
in the cup in my fingers, not waiting,
meeting no one

Fever

Our dreams the surfeit
imagination of a natural world,
its turkey grass picked to cure our fever, white flower
culled in August
& hung upside down in branches to dry
The flies drunk on it, full of flu
Our dreams are gravel trucks cutting up the hill road
where your house is sinking deeper, trucks moving
the county from one edge to the lakeshore,
tipping it.
The pommes pourries chatter in the branches,
two *chks* & a whistle, red-winged
blackbird.
Behind the house, dogged raspberries that never bear.
Their heads shut off & they
won't be speaking.
Maybe ever.

At night in the dream, a red truck
comes to take the house away,
its dumper full of dirt to fill the hole in.
Only the house is barn-shaped, not our real house,
its windows impermeable to light
We are outside it, sleeping in the dark spikes of
timothy
In our bedroom there are are grey moths pushing the wool urge
of their wings onto sticky paper.

& the truck carries off little pieces. Cutting its engine.
To the lakeshore. Where the fever is. The water.
The raspberries watching.
Just like that.

Four Propositions for Climate

It's the wood & paint of the chairs
speak loudest,
when we are not wearing them.
Where the grass stops at the edge of desert.
Trying as if for the first time, on the lawn, the
fault-lines of the heart
where two continents fit & push overboard
touching

the sky with our mouths & no damn chatter ever.
Bless us this day thy fairly grain
forgive us our name & address thy chair
among us,
emptied by clutter & rain, what if.

Green the plant colour, made of light.
Green the artesian water after the week of storm.
White chairs on the new-cut lawn.
Your blue sweater bunched up in the garden
& you in it, squatting over lettuce.
In our glasses, small drunk
insects, pickled & glad.
Our way of verbs, excessive
Badlands left in us from the old seas, where the ice
broke down, & receded

Wood & paint of the chairs speak loudest,
undercut by the dig dig
of your hand between peas & broccoli
That fault-line, where two continents
stop
because their villages are fragile, not
built to earthquake standards
The fault-line of the heart, where two continents
Fit.
This road, or any road. Into the desert. & after that.
Where we are sitting. What if

The Wings

As if everything were smooth
As if every life wore down the edges of our pictures
until our hands touched
& we kissed between the frames

from your silence where our hands speak
& silence is, instead, inside our shoulders
the clavicle hollow as a bird's wings
holding the arms in place
My kiss caught in its mouth of sky
My kiss sucking its harsh beat rushed my tongue inside
like a wing rising
A wing inside my ear

Your gentleness is also a hurting
a worn kiss closing its mouth
I long for
The cicadas
Those wings   singing high-pitched raw silver light boots rising
Until I am peaceful, until my face shuts up &
remembers you, the edge of the picture worn, where we leaked out
& our arms touched
& scared us
The wings of the cicadas
Heard in the field from any direction
Our wings

That small

Hooked

Some times we didn't know how hooked we were,
your hands in the dishwater,
you watching
the red shirt moving down the road at Dubois' barn,
light of late afternoon makes your eyes
shine from any direction,
as in those old paintings of saints
whose eyes follow the viewer,
brutal wounds on their bodies bleeding
perfect drops from the thorn

Some times I am still looking for jazz on the radio,
still buying the daily paper,
reading crossword clues & horoscopes,
not answering any questions.

If all the words in us could come as cleanly,
the small squares & interlocking pattern!

Our voices across the brown table are
talking serious fear,
the erosion of personal space:
fear of the pig-boy on his motorcycle,
the ladies of the *rang* taking their night walk up the road,
answering or not answering your greeting,
do they recognize you, your loveliness,
the small saintedness of your body

Some times we didn't know how hooked we were,
on one or the other side of the neighbours,
eating dinner,
your eyes following me whether or not
you are really looking,
the small wound you bear because of my furious glances,
our embrace beside the sink & cupboards,
trying to kiss each other in a house bright
as an aquarium,
the red shirt of the neighbour moving,
walking into the barn where we knew there were cows,
heavy from waiting

Ocean Poem

I am the one who lies, slowly, closer
to your arm.
I insinuate.
The trip trip of the rain into wet earth &
the traffic noise.
This kind of a hush[1], she said.
Lifting her arms over her head so gently
in a gesture of, longing.
We are all innocent beings with our bathtubs[2] & literary
pure enforcement.
I don't know if there's any difference between men & women[3]
is just a lie.[4]
The word human being has stood for men
until now.

Until now.

When she puts her arm down, in innocence, [5]
I'll show her.[6]

---

[1] *There's a kind of a hush, all over the world, tonight*
All over the world, you can hear the sound of lovers in love.
        —Herman's Hermits, 1966

[2] Places to get clean. Large, enamel, clumsy. "Bathtub gin".

[3] The poets who say this believe that the standard of poetic excellence is just excellent & not male.

[4] This should not be done in any poem, accusing someone of lying.

[5] In no sense.

[6] Read "shore". This is an ocean poem.

In These (Tough) Times

I want to say just now I don't care
about the three fish lying on the counter
their stomachs opened in a straight line
soft & waiting for the pan

to heat up

I want to say just now I don't care
The rockets above my building are testing
Russian overcoats
The traffic stops at the light where two streets
meet head-on
A design problem

I want to say just now I don't care
The fat in the pan is smoking
The grey shadow of my thought rises
I want to carry my body restless into your room
& hold my mouth beside your ear
where I first kissed you
"beyond consequence"

Tho your body (out of pain) remembers only painfulness
just yet
I want to say just now I can live
without jubilance
I want to say I'm never again going to be lonely
I want you to sleep

as I lay the fish soft into the frypan
& smell the fat cooling
& hear the crackle of the fish skin
cooking

to feed you
When you wake up & call me
If you call me
The light in the courtyard making
the lace on your long window
tremble

As I do
lifting the fish up
to turn them

Unfurled & Dressy

Frontally speaking
I am facing up to my harbingers
I am wearing a small beam to stop from
measuring the sky
I am approaching my debits
with a voice left from the Elections
A yelp
The start of a cry

Frontally speaking I am leaning on the hugest boulder
by the wayside
in order to imprint the mountain on my ass
In order to jump into the abyss with my shoes named Kafka
In order to complete the fire escape of my marriage

Frontally speaking I am no more important
than the construction of a stadium
in the place where they refused to build
housing for the poor
I have inside me
no less sky than the sky

Frontally speaking my sadness wears another seven
beside your opportunity
It is unfurled & dressy
It is your voice which I am speaking over & over
because I like to hear you
inside my mouth
where I can touch our futures with my tongue
& throw down my names & embrace you
& forget which one of us I am
Frontally speaking
Frontally speaking

Three Signs

Her absence as real as presence,
as anyone's presence.
She is the small woman in a plane above Castlegar,
worrying each rivet,
will it stay intact in the wing.
In her memory film how some of us are laughing
self-consciously,
pretending to find some thing in the bushes,
making the thrashing sound on purpose,
half this & half bluster.
Did you see us.

Down by the ocean park above the rockface, sea birds eating up the tide,
sun burnt in the surface of the water
Huge trunk of the coastal giant we touched
that would make X many houses,
& had a sign counting them

until the Pope's visit.
When the city sought to make the homeless vanish
by taking signs down,

thinking the words alone inciteful

2

I want to give the characteristic whelp or yelp
that says I've found something.
Imagine that.

If there's one thing I learned from marriage
it was talking sweet
to policemen.
He'd leave with them so meek they'd think I was crazy when
I'd phoned them.
My word against his.
Imagine *that.*

3

Any minute now the woman's plane will land in Castlegar
& she'll go by road up the Slocan Valley
which is a beautiful name after all.
Worried about her speeches but astonished at the Western trees.
I just hope she hears me listening
in the clear Coastal light she flew from
The sign of her presence, craving

I just hope she's warm

Miss Chatelaine

In the movie, the horse almost dies.
A classic for children, where the small girl pushes a thin
knife into the horse's side.
Later I am sitting in brightness with the women
I went to high school with in Calgary,
fifteen years later we are all feminist, talking of the girl
in the film.
The horse who has some parasite & is afraid of the storm,
& the girl who goes out to save him.
We are in a baggage car on VIA Rail around a huge table,
its varnish light & cold,
as if inside the boardrooms of the corporation;
the baggage door is open
to the smell of dark prairie,
we are fifteen years older, serious
about women, these images:
the girl running at night between the house & the barn,
& the noise of the horse's fear mixed in with the rain.

Finally there are no men between us.
Finally none of us are passing or failing according to
Miss Chatelaine.
I wish I could tell you how much I love you,
my friends with your odd looks, our odd looks,
our nervousness with each other,
the girl crying out as she runs in the darkness,
our decoration we wore, so many years ago, high school
boys watching from another table.

Finally I can love you.
Wherever you have gone to, in your secret marriages.
When the knife goes so deeply into the horse's side, a
few seconds & the rush of air.
In the morning, the rain is over.
The space between the house & barn is just a space again.
Finally I can meet with you & talk this over.
Finally I can see us meeting, & our true tenderness, emerge.

Furious

Culinary

If people could eat ashes would anyone be hungry
If people could eat road runoff would they feel memory's
absence
Would people eat poetry could I write it fast enough
Would I ever
Would anyone hear me if I rolled over in the middle
of their dream
Should I cancel my ticket
Should I come anyway & take a bus into the centre of the city
Would anyone bring my suitcase from the attic
it is so heavy
it is full of birds
it is full of a small meadow
it is full of work
it is spelled wurq here & remember this
I am tired of wurqing
I am tired of handwriting the alphabet there are only
26 characters
I am tired of characters
I am going my plane is there

Are you coming with my suitcase
Are you coming with my hair combed in the manner of
the highest table
You are taking too long my ticket is old
& forgets its airplane
Should I come anyhow
Will I be able to remember the name of my ticket
if anyone asks me
Will my sandwich portray me exactly in all my history
If there were enough ashes would anyone be hungry
Would the alphabet shut up I've had enough now go away from me
It's working
Sayonara, αντιο, thank you for your trouble,
where can I change money, bring me coca-cola,
don't worry, I'm fine

The Producers

What the producers do to meat, you pay for in your cells.
It is your cells I have come to speak about.
Only a certain thickness separates me from the air in this room.
Density. Its whirligig spinning
to the tune of bouzouki music.
My body the street fair offers you the altered clothing of the cells.
It offers you the chance to read a novel by a famous woman
in which other women reproduce, & their
value is this:
reproduction.

It is because of this I have come to speak to you:
because it is possible that
the meaning of a woman is the meaning of a single cell.

A certain thickness prevents me from saying what I might say.
The difference between a human cell & the atoms in this table.
I lean my head against the wood.
Where are you, I want to speak to you.
What the producers do to lettuce, you pay for in your cells.
Everything they do, you will pay for.
Your cells will not recognize what they are to become.
It is on behalf of your cells.
I speak to you without election because the cells know nothing
of democracy.
They think not of the good of the whole, but of themselves.
They think of their thin unguarded border.
The illusion of wholeness captivates us, as a kind of slavery.
I asked a woman with cancer, who told me.
Now she has died because some cells wanted to go
someplace else.
Before she died, she thought about the producers
of x-rays,
& how we once believed we could see thru anything,
we humans.

Acceptances

I accept your 14 complaints about the body. I accept your 7
memories. I accept your 4 tricks with cards, where the Kings rise to
the top when you knock on the deck, the Queens are found together
in the middle (the trick of the burning building), the aces vanish.

& the 4th one, where the cards appear in order after the storm strews
light across the house-front, tearing the white blind.

Clubs, hearts, diamonds, spades.
The queens with their single eyes & desexed dresses, their legs
gone, become the head of their own image,
their twin.
& the knaves & kings, similar.

I accept your 14 complaints about the body. The head emerging
from both ends of the torso. The hands ending in the air, 4 fingers
of air locked with the fingers of the hand. Breath is here. Breath is
breathing in the hands when you shuffle the cards, now the aces

are separate, the joker has gone back into the burning building
to unlock the queens, who are married

to each other. Which is your 14th complaint about the body. They
married each other. You had to get back out
down the stairs alone, & fall,
cauterized, into the embrace of the firemen.

9 Maps to Dreams Where Rats are Seen

We long for, the rat fondles our chest & forehead.

The hand of the rat waving goodbye.

The part of the rat in our mouth, tasting like the hand.

The rat, fondling us in our deepest hand.

At the back of the restaurant, the rat is sitting, his howl standing up his rough, disobedient fur.

The part of the rat howls.

Rats as a star, she said. Rats as a star.

Name of the fur.

Her old coat her skin shutting out the howl.

Patron

Well well he said his hands
up on his face push the slow skin dissolve frame over sunlight
the window over his shoulder where cold air blast is
stopped & he is speaking, well well he said
you are well hired & working here
to do this work so calmly
& learn the hierarchy as you will
need us he said well well he speak & push his face & grin
the office tower over airless
the office tower in which we discuss over airless
the air unbreak between us over every
well he said
to do this so calmly
I will not, she said
I will/not

He held up his hands so we could see the handcuffs.
He stepped off the plane & held up the handcuffs so we could see his
hands.
Out of the small white-painted plane he stepped & raised his arms so
we could see the handcuffs on his hands.
Out of the small plane rivetted carefully by union labour & painted white
he raised his hands with the cuffs on them.
So we could see his hands locked together with the handcuffs he stepped
out of the plane holding his arms upward.
When the plane landed, three RCMP entered & emerged with him in
handcuffs.

On the tarmac he was escorted by the RCMP.
On the tarmac after stepping out of the small plane painted white with
his arms in the air so we could see the handcuffs he was escorted by
the RCMP.
When the plane landed, the RCMP entered it & emerged with him.
Before he stepped into the car he waved his hands so we could see.

Breakneck Speeed

Soft fall of the grasses.
A boy sleeping under the huge breath of his tiger.
The disgraced American president Nixon
in our history books
played only the piano, & stared up seriously
in his white shirt
at a tin bird on the wall above the sheet-music.
Thou are the rock of ages, stand by me, he sang
in the picture.
The white crease of the shirt on Nixon's arm,
his mouth open.
So what.
So bloody what.
A grass fire can eat up everything, including
fences.
These are brain-markers, too,
the line between properties in the head,
between what we think we know, &
what happened.
Nothing happened.
Take my word for it.
Krushchev, Eisenhower, Elvis, Roosevelt, & Stalin.
Or ask General Patton.

If you ask me, I'm getting
outa here at breakneck speeed.

Muddy Thinking

To be found, guilty of it
To be found guilty of it, a package on the desk
to think with, not *memory* but

Think with this, says the label

& she opens it & it's just mud.
Mud is good for
      a) the complexion
      b) hut walls
      c) cooling the feet of donkeys

In Legourion at the roadside taverna where the owner brushed off
the dust of tour buses from the table with his apron, making all of us
filthy with his welcome, & bringing us cold Amstel to lay the dust
down in our throats, the woman on the donkey approaching, the
donkey carrying the woman & a load of sticks tied up with burlap,
the woman so black hitting hola hola the donkey with one stick & it
stops right in front of us to defecate, the woman switching wildly &
cursing Christos for her misfortune stuck in front of these Canadians
& her donkey is shitting, curse it Christos, the sun beating down,

You're heading for a fall, said Aline to me when we argued
on the bus back to Nauplion

& three years later when I passed the same restaurant on another
trip, the tables now piled against a wall & just a small boy in green
sweater selling *portokolada* from a metal cooler in the dust & the
road empty

The day after my birthday I couldn't breathe & didn't think anything
of it just walked slower & slower & stayed out of monuments

Until the hospital in Athens with emergency in one room & all the
Greeks worried smoking including the doctors who decided I was
from Belgium or Toronto
& Fifty people from Legourion have emigrated to Toronto
the woman in the field told me, looking up from the half-planted
furrow & gave me directions: past that hill, she said, is Europe:

Corrections to Muddy Thinking

You're heading for a fall, said Aline to me when we argued human justice
me laughing full of the beer

The two women I was travelling with gone back to Nauplion
where festival streamers flutter from the lamps & lambs hang head down
in the butchers', soft snouts streaming blood like syrup on the marble
counter

The day after my birthday I couldn't breathe & didn't think anything
of it just walked slower & slower & stayed out of monuments
thinking it a psychological withdrawal or
acute loneliness
& made it to Athens where in the crowded odos on the way to the
hospital my face was hit by the flank of a lamb carried over some-
one's shoulder startling me with its cold peeled body wearing
ribbons

Vous avez la bronchite, madame, the doctor told me gravely

& gave me medicine with speed in it banned in North America

The woman in the field who saw me walking so slow on the
road-edge & cried out Toronto! Toronto! recognizing my peculiar
uptight walk, & gave me directions I never asked for, the way country
people give directions pointing perfectly but never saying how far
anything is, distance not being important in the present tense

& me not caring at all where Europe was since I could hardly breathe
at that exact moment & if I wasn't in Europe already then where was I

Wearing the Map of Africa

The hurt mouth full of dust, crying to dream.
I take you in my arms like oranges or diamonds or wine.
On television the South African riots are processions
for the rioted dead; policemen
with peaked caps & rifles who look like the army
not the police
fire into the crowd.
These funerals have to stop, say the ruling party,
they've gone past mourning the dead.
Singing freedom songs, the black marchers dancing
in the road kick the tear gas bombs farther away,
or back at the armed men.
The government is trying restore calm, the voice says;
calm, what is this word with its four deaf ciphers
& small beak

The National network bringing this film clip to you,
the white cameraman, of course, benefitting from
exactly what he portrays
He is so invisible we can see outward from his beak
Oh how white he is
The day has many colours
This poem is white too
Oh how white I am

Does the word *restore* mean anything?
The word *calm*?

The tear gas cannister & the dancing man lifting his arms
up, his jacket lifting, the map of Africa
on his t-shirt, & behind him
a woman, the map of Africa on her t-shirt,
& behind her, another man, the map of Africa on
his t-shirt, & behind, another, the map of Africa on her
t-shirt, wearing the map of Africa,
the shape of Africa

The word calm means suppressed anger.
The word calm means implode.
The word restore means suppress anger.
The word means where does anger go to when its beak is
shut, forcibly
Where does the anger go to it doesn't go anywhere
We are still dancing
We are still dancing
the word is angry, angry
It has gone beyond mourning the dead.
It is honouring the living.
It is honouring the mouth, hurt,
trying to dream.

My arms are oranges, soft juice bitter sweet & that beautiful colour.
Orange is indescribable apart from that sweetness.
My beak is shut. It is the colour of sweetness
I am trying to dream

Salt: Condition

When I held up the small wriggling animal in my hands
in the dream
it was my tongue, I had torn it out
by accident, it was loosely rooted.

The bark of the tree, under which pulses thin syrup.

A world where there are these beginnings & no more:
the salt upon the table in its cellar
the coat of dust on the tongue & a few threads of the sweater
bright blue, laid beside each other.

I hid my hands with the tongue still wriggling, got up
from the wedding & went into the bathroom which was
huge & white as in high school, where the young women
smoke together & feel their bodies growing,
apart from each other, secretly, alone.

The tree from which the bird tears small bugs & searches for its
nest, which it has lost now, unable to concentrate.

The salt is poured onto the chests of the newly dead to
taketh away their sins.

With both hands I tried to push back the tongue,
its torn end, unravelled like a sweater.

What else I abhor.

Above everything.

That year, two of my high school friends cried & said they were
pregnant, then vanished,
the washroom left empty.

The tongue struggled out of my fingers, a bird
whose nest was touched by humans, its eggs pecked
ragged in its fright,
the young leaked out & ruined.

Above everything.

& afterward, be afraid, unable to concentrate.

Where the mouth is.

Pure Writing is a Notion Beyond the Pen

All of this an avoidance of the script:
the small turquoise shirt rolled up over the shoulders, the narrow
angle of sun in the yard, the body, the body,
oh, the body
with its view of the cold dew on the grass this morning, silver,
like a ring
Dreaming over & over of
women's madness, my mother's madness, the madness of
the neighbour woman shut up in High River,
where I was caught in a blizzard once, drifts choking the road & cars

until there is no anger any longer.
Until none of us is angry,
until our women's faces are the blindness of snow & refract light
until our house is so lit it has the sound of steel
until light becomes the absence of weight
& does not resemble us any longer

My brother out in his long yard stooped beside the haybine,
the thin swath of clover & timothy
drying in the sun, & the narrow muscle in his back, his head
completely vanished

into a place where there is no more childhood, just
the heat of August risen off New Holland equipment,
the connection   between   things & things,
the air hose & the tractor

air hose

tractor

In spite of us, the connection
between words, are words things, are they names of things,
the speed of light notwithstanding,
why do we go mad & forget everything, & be unable to speak of it,
as if: pure writing is a notion beyond the pen
she said, & held her head to keep the wind in,
& named it this

Three Versions

"Why do you have to choose
a definitive version?"
                        —Gail Scott

(1)

Sometimes you can't tell
if the bird's wings have been beaten shut
or just bitten off or its chest
eaten, sucked in, or
if the stone has fallen from
the wet sky into its mouth,
or if the shell had torn the skin at birth, leaking the air in,
or if the poet has written with
or without discipline.

(2)

Sometimes you can't tell
if the bird's wings have been beaten shut
or just bitten off & it won't fly, or its chest
eaten, sucked in, or
if the stone has fallen from
the wet sky into its mouth,
making the song a bit of a surprise finally,
sometimes you can't tell where the bird's lungs
end & the sky begins,
or if the shell had torn the skin at birth, leaking the air in,
or if the poet has written with
or without discipline.

(3)

Sometimes you can't tell
if the bird's wings have been beaten shut
or garbaged,
or just bitten off & it won't fly, or its chest burned
with white stove matches, or
eaten, sucked in, or
if the stone has fallen from
the wet sky into its mouth,
making the song a bit of a surprise finally,
a song with a rock in it,
a small marble,
sometimes you can't tell where the bird's lungs
end & the sky begins, its wings dash too quickly,
or if the shell had torn the skin at birth, leaking the air in,
or if the script of flight is a membrane in the head, or
just shut into the long bones,
or what it feels like exactly to have a beak, where
the mouth is, impossible to tell you this,
or if the poet has written with
or without discipline.

Betty

O darkness & the empty moons, women
speaking light words into the cups of each other's fingers.
Or the mouth that fills a whole room, whispering
black air, not saliva, & not im/
pertinence.
We are here forever, unspoken, our undershirts stick in the room's heat,
stick between the breasts, in the flat place over the bone
that holds the chest
from tearing open, like the metal traps' cold tensity
where we laid them rusted in the city river,
drown-set for muskrat
Our small hands frozen, without fingers, claws of ice holding stiff snouts of fur
strange sprung words leaking

into our sentences.
"A-girls", the 2 year old girl called out at the supper table.
Let's not say "Grace" again, she said, let's say "Betty".
In the second public grade of school there were
5 Johns & 3 Debbies, 3 Darlenes, 2 Tims,
most of them grew up called Didi or Evan, & I stared out the window
at the racks of bicycles, tipped any way over, flat prairie line-scape,
the one consistent image I have of school.

Why are so many women lonely, empty as the inside of bicycles, as
the mouths using all the room,
the boys in their tight jeans &
slimness that will leave them in their 22nd year,
the boys & their hard laugh who is tougher,
boys getting at each other's love, thru the inside
of women, their intermediary, their confessional.

I want to speak sexually of one thing–not male love
but physical knowing: the distance
between the breastbone & the palm, the two
important parts of the body.
Where the water runs in the long veins, curving thru space.
The palm where you can dive in & drink & never come up again,
& forgive no one, & feel, as you break the surface–
your head wet, streaming, smelling faintly of milk or oranges

Gorgeous

In any case, what are our chances.
In any case, whatsoever our chances, finally, where.
At the end of this century.
At the beginning, middle, or end of this century.
The hay baler coiled in the yard, with its square bales of hay.
The woman upstairs on the bed, listless.
Her cells are inscribed with the secret code given her at her birth, squeezed
out of the walls of her mother.
Her cells are inscribed with the small coils of the chromosomes,
defining her motion, the possible range,
even the books she has written,
down to the last letter.
One heart tick on the narrow screen pulled down this evening
for the moving picture of the heart.
The moving entity.
Blood-flow, gorging the ventricles, the chambers with their small colours,
that colour, pain's orange
light between the bulbs of the fingers, so unlike daylight, hidden
in the capillaries of the hands.
The woman who touches her hair.
Who touches, every month, her own blood.
This expiation of the body, not petty, but, *critical*.
A snake has come to my water-trough.
The narrow sip of water falling into my lungs.
If I shouted, who among the hierarchy of angels would hear me, these words.
& failing that.
What are our chances.
What are our chances.
If our cancer can be removed without fear, under local conditions.
The chromosomes unrolled & kissed,
until they are better.

& the woman gets out of the bed.
The blood on her legs, overflowing the small stopper.
The bird risen in the branches.
In what book, concealed, is its name.
I river, I river, I river.
Trust the verb.
Motion.
In the line, too, motion.
I love you. The book is ended.
The blood gorges gorges gorges the bed.

2. THE ACTS

compression. To use a kind of compression, so compressed that the
links between the image/phrases break down, but the whole poem
still retains its connection.

inter-text. Using and repeating my own and others' earlier texts.
Pulling the old poems thru the new, making the old lines a thread
thru the eye of the words I am sewing. Sound & sense. The eeriness.

everyday event. Must take and use the everyday connection between
things. Not talking a philosophical language. Watching terminol-
ogy. Make the compression so hard that it functions as terminology,
and I can just use the ordinary words in their street clothes.

physical body. Image of the whole physical body must always be
there. Not truncated, not synecdoche, but the physical image speak-
ing directly the entire body at once

Combining the colloquial expression with the words of intellect. In one poem. To show how when counterpointed it is those colloquial expressions that are contextually the most pure. & at the same time so idiotic we must laugh. This is juxtaposed.

I am tired of the same old interrelated logic of the signs that we insist upon as if it were true. Ain't true. Truly. True blew.

The slow singing of the evangelicals outside my door, their linguistic intrusion. There are days I want to give up my head. To whom am I being charitable. To whom will I offer it?

It's the way people use language makes me furious. The ones who reject the colloquial & common culture. The ones who laud on the other hand the common & denigrate the intellect, as if we are not thinking. The ones who play between the two, as if culture is a strong wind blowing in the path of *honour*. It takes us nowhere & makes me furious, that's all.

The poems are called **Pure Reason**.

BECAUSE pure reason in the end is beyond all logic, and beyond the signs. Logic is just something imposed upon reason. It's one kind of connectedness, that creates points of conjunction and reference that may not be true, & may not have helped us much as human beings in the end (and certainly not as women). From where we are now.

PURE REASON is, of its essence, UNreasonable; it can't be itself reasoned or it wouldn't be pure reason. PURE REASON is the source of our reasonableness; our reasonableness (which may or may not be "reasonable") is its flaw. A leak. An uncontrolled space, at the edge. Where the so-called "purity" is already broken.

PURE REASON would be the source of Intelligibility, and Cause too. It must have to do with love, at its root. No matter how it is obliterated after that.

The perfect flatness of ordinary language, our ordinary saying of it, radio & electrodes, to use this flat surface to open the deep emotional current that lies just beneath its surface, that some people deny because the surface is so flat.

This emotional current is pure reason. <u>Before</u> reasoning. Before the <u>word</u> "reasoning", which is only a <u>social</u> convention and has nothing to do with pure reason at all. It contains the ordinary flat language, but not necessarily the converse. The ordinary language is just a surface pushed up & flat from underneath. This surface is not "content" in the same way that we normally use the word "content". It can be form, as well.

How in the poem the animals hold the emotional current and are a vessel for it, carrying it through two time zones. Because the poem is not about animals at all, but about the fantasies of the audience, and this content lies under the flat surface of the poem. So that the <u>surface content</u> is actually <u>a form</u> for the real emotional "content" of the poem.

To do this again. To keep this door open & my hands in it, writing. Making the voice speak what the hands have already spoken. The embrace, before the utterance.

Always.

We're talking about two different things. Taking a lot of common
locutions & using them over & broken in the piece, the sound o̶f
them being important, and the sense not at all. Because everyo̶
knows what they mean & refer to. The poem doesn't have to d̶

As in what ancient ways: the opening up of sense percepti̶
opening of the powers to heal. Referentiality distorts m̶
conveys, it injects us with the comfortable. I crave ins̶
that "act within a context but do not refer to it" ̶
Technicians of the Sacred).

ne surface then what
e depth or is it
r thought.
line if written
moving.

naunts me on the surface
Be lyric. In my image. In my
with the mouth pushed shut...

on is an
re than it
ead images
Rothenberg,

efer.

pth" under the surface is NOT the culture that
ge, inherited from the visible only. It is behind that.
s behind or are we excellent beings.

sexual. If our "depth" is choked at the surface, becomes a sexual problem. Lady MacB. saying ye gods unsex me now. Where our female sex is without consequence we must cast it off to act, to speak. Or wear the cast the culture offers us: the surface of the page.

The blind calf with the membrane over its head, tottering in the darkness, the wall of the house near it, it feels the warmth of indoor heating. The membrane choking in its mouth, should it choose to eat it? Its mother still labours, giving birth to its twin. Smaller, lighter, shrivelled. If the blind calf lives it is because it learned inside its mother to take that space from its own twin. Inside the womb. Where it was so dark, does it ever need vision again?

The A List

The Outlander Gil Adamson
The Circle Game Margaret Atwood
Power Politics Margaret Atwood
Second Words Margaret Atwood
Survival Margaret Atwood
These Festive Nights Marie-Claire Blais
La Guerre Trilogy Roch Carrier
The Hockey Sweater and Other Stories Roch Carrier
Hard Core Logo Nick Craine
Great Expectations Edited by Dede Crane and Lisa Moore
Queen Rat Lynn Crosbie
The Honeyman Festival Marian Engel
The Bush Garden Northrop Frye
Eleven Canadian Novelists Interviewed by Graeme Gibson
Five Legs Graeme Gibson
Death Goes Better with Coca-Cola Dave Godfrey
Technology and Empire George Grant
De Niro's Game Rawi Hage
Kamouraska Anne Hébert
Ticknor Sheila Heti
No Pain Like This Body Harold Sonny Ladoo
Civil Elegies Dennis Lee
Mermaids and Ikons Gwendolyn MacEwen
Ana Historic Daphne Marlatt
Like This Leo McKay Jr.
Selected Short Fiction of Lisa Moore
Selected Poems Alden Nowlan
Poems for all the Annettes Al Purdy
Manual for Draft-Age Immigrants to Canada Mark Satin
The Little Girl Who Was Too Fond of Matches Gaetan Soucy
Made for Happiness Jean Vanier
Basic Black with Pearls Helen Weinzweig
Passing Ceremony Helen Weinzweig
The Big Why Michael Winter
This All Happened Michael Winter

Then if the surface haunts me. If there is a name <u>surface</u> then what else is there. Is what is "different" from the surface <u>depth</u> or is it <u>another surface</u>. The language imposes dualism on our thought. Which must be broken, so to, speak. *How when the line if written there is blank page below, into which the signs are moving.*

Can I, in writing the next line, refuse what haunts me on the surface of the page, with its easy affirmation. *Be lyric. In my image. In my image. Forty lifetimes in the desert with the mouth pushed shut...*

The emotional "depth" under the surface is NOT the culture that occupies the p ge, inherited from the visible only. It is behind that. Either we p s behind or are we excellent beings.

   sexual. If our "depth" is choked at the surface, becomes a sexual problem. Lady MacB. saying ye gods unsex me now. Where our female sex is without consequence we must cast it off to act, to speak. Or wear the cast the culture offers us: the surface of the page.

The blind calf with the membrane over its head, tottering in the darkness, the wall of the house near it, it feels the warmth of indoor heating. The membrane choking in its mouth, should it choose to eat it? Its mother still labours, giving birth to its twin. Smaller, lighter, shrivelled. If the blind calf lives it is because it learned inside its mother to take that space from its own twin. Inside the womb. Where it was so dark, does it ever need vision again?

We're talking about two different things. Taking a lot of common locutions & using them over & broken in the piece, the sound of them being important, and the sense not at all. Because everyone knows what they mean & refer to. The poem doesn't have to defer.

As in what ancient ways: the opening up of sense perception is an opening of the powers to heal. Referentiality distorts more than it conveys, it injects us with the comfortable. I crave instead images that "act within a context but do not refer to it" (Rothenberg, *Technicians of the Sacred*).

What is key to this desire: To have one's existence affirmed by others. Or, put oneself at risk forever (a panic at the cell's edge). Or is it affirmation, first, that then makes the risk possible? To bear it. The risk of, kissing her.

The embrace first, then the utterance.

What this need for affirmation meant before was having an existence affirmed by men. Knowing how they praise well what affirms their relation. They do not have to put them-selves at risk, which women have always had to do, to exist, to speak, to have their existence affirmed by others.

What I had not spoken! The way she cried out because of my silence, & how I chose it, stubborn. My defense of necessity. Because my eyes and my whole body could see that the words and bodies of women were not listened to or affirmed.

But we women listen so carefully to each other. The resurrection of the woman's body is of Kore, not the phallic king-dom. This affirmation is the true necessity. To inhabit freely the civic house of memory I am kept out of.

Oh!

What that surface is still haunts me. The people who move in the surface of the poem, becoming signs. Are they form or content.

They are not the real content. And in my loneliness, for days I am breathing brother air, my brothers outside throwing the football, the wall they are throwing it over is the huge gap between us. It is just air.

I think of the people who go around carrying the scars on their arms that they have made for themselves. It is defiance of the real. It is saying you can defy reality by mutilating your skin (that surface). As if your own physical matter is the place where you can leak outside of the real. It is a refusal of desire (at which point, do we not refuse memory too?).

The poet, instead, defies "real"-ity by writing it hard into the pages, building that surface (content), as a form wherein she makes her defiance visible. (The "real-" that women have never inhabited as whole beings: it has never been formed by our desire, Irigaray says.)

I want to write these things like *Unfurled & Dressy* that can't be torn apart by anybody, anywhere, or in the university. I want the overall sound to be one of making sense, but I don't want the inside of the poem to make sense of anything.

People who are making sense are just making me laugh, is all.

& If the three parts of the poem are "disconnected" only because of the way we read. Their connection being neither logical nor purely associative but involving instead a giant leap in & out of the "event" that makes the surface of the poem. I want those kind of transitions wherein there's a kind of leap that's *parallel* to the rest of the poem. Where the parts are seemingly unrelated but can't exist without each other.

There's no way you can logically or symptomatically break down & explain the connection between these parts. But, yet, when you take two parallel things & place them in the same reading, you enunciate a kind of alteration: your perception of one part is affected by your perception of the others, whether you like it or not. &, I believe anyhow, that there are connections between seemingly parallel things that haven't been enunciated yet because of flaws or "closed sets" (flaws is a value judgement) in our ways of speech. So, then, do we give up? Or do we try to break open the connections in another way?

What I am trying to do in my work these days is two things: 1) break down the logical connections/structure of "meaning" (referentiality), and 2) break down the noun/verb opposition wherein the present so-called 'power' of the language resides, both of these while still using the surface of ordinary speaking as a reflex for emotional power…

To break down the noun/verb opposition that is a kind of absolut-
ism in the language itself. So that using the words affirms, <u>no matter</u>
<u>what</u>, the dominant Order.

That the noun and verb possess the strength, power, force in
language has been ingrained in us from our earliest school. The
signs for <u>object</u>/<u>names</u>, and the signs for the <u>movement</u> of these
objects. This re/presents <u>reality.</u> The thing & the act. Space, & time.

<u>To try to move the force in language from the noun/verb centre</u>. To
de/centralize the force inside the utterance from the <u>noun</u>/<u>verb</u>, say,
to the <u>preposition</u>. Even for a moment. To break the vertical hold.
To empower the preposition to signify and utter motion, the motion
of the utterance, and thereby <u>Name.</u>

The Motion before the Name.

If the preposition can disturb the force of the utterance and phrase: this changes reading. Like the eye reads the TV screen: the screen's multiplicity of repetition creates the image for us, the image not <u>On the screen</u> but embedded IN the repetitions. The THING we are seeing is a MOTION. The Motion <u>before</u> the Name. The image/ thing is not <u>object</u> but <u>act.</u> Not act, but act act act—a continual relation.

If we can read the page as the eye reads the screen. The act of speaking it. The kind of motion that our eyes read not Verb-al, but Preposition-al. <u>On across under toward</u> us...

It is the force of the <u>preposition</u> that alters place! Can its dis-placement of the noun/verb dis-place also <u>naming</u>, dis-placing reality? Even momentarily. Make a fissure through which we can leak out from the "real" that is sewn into us, to utter what could not be uttered in the previous structure. Where we have not been represented, except through **Dominant** (in this case, patriarchal) speaking, which even we speak, even we women.

Just as a new particle entering a field alters the position and force of particles already present (even when the particle entering is the writer's eye), this fissure and our leaking through it can alter the relation of the noun/verb in the utterance, the relation not of MEANING but of the FORCE of language, in a way that cannot properly be predicted.

First change the Motion (force), then this will alter Naming (mean-ing). Because it is the force of language that maintains the power of its naming. In this way, the patriarchal structure (way-of-naming) of language, masculine language, is maintained by the noun/verb force. The same way certain stresses (which are "motions") hold up buildings. Whether or not we choose it.

To put the weight of the utterance on the preposition, or even to let the preposition enter the field "out of order", changes this. Creates, what sounds like, a stutter. To the trained ear. Our "well-trained" ears.

To take the movement of the eye that is <u>seeing</u>, and use it to make the reading surface of the poem.

On the radio, the arrival of the exiled terrorist who is an ordinary human who was so angry twenty years ago, how the description highlights the raised arms and handcuffs, you hear it on the morning news every 10 minutes, those two physical details. Because they are, in the end, what is important; there is no "event" apart from the handcuffs. In a painting this is where there would be the most light, right where the handcuffs are. If not light, then darkness. Or a skull and an open book, a tree, a leaf. Or ciphers from tombs, iconic. *Guil Apol.*

And the eye would transmit this light message to the brain over and over. As if we are looking at a painting; as if the eye is looking for the first time, curious, at a painting or photograph, the rapid movement of its gaze transmits the surface to us, until either the real becomes abstracted, or the abstraction of light on the page becomes real. And the handcuffs themselves are marks of punctuation, bearing the two dark commas of the hands.

The poem is not called "Terrorist" because "terrorist" is a word conferred by those who have already taken power. The poem is about the exile, who is not what is terrible. It is the co-incidence of the police like an embrace. And the bracelets.

The verb moves forward or backward in time, erasing everything behind it. Contains in itself *narration*. The verb tells a story because it walks off & the noun just hangs on! Dear life!

But the preposition, & what is prepositional, shows not motion or name but the relation between thing & act, defines space <u>and</u> time, by relation-ship. Without naming. Without erasing. Before & into. Without itself moving ever. Because it is "part of" & not separate.

The match stays lit & does not flicker. When the woman comes to from sedation & electroshock, who will she be then. That electro-effort to instill motion. & she stays, neither name nor motion: pre-position-al.

The relation drove her mad. Motion & name *matter*. The problem with the preposition is, *no inflection. Time & space, but an unvalued grammatical relation. Seen as a dependency, rather than recognized as a value: the space between over before, by.* As if the preposition is the woman's sign because it is relational. But can't get anywhere, because in the language it has no power, & can't exist alone.

No wonder she went away. No wonder the cars were obliterated by snow. Remember, Marianne? Both of us in the Fort McLeod police station, midnight, asking when they'd open the road.

Is it impossible to conceptualize (in English) without using "the thing"? Our language that objectifies TIME (i.e. the words "phase", "touch", which are really relations, not things) is one that supports easily the hegemony of "singleness", "individual power", "phallus". Its thingness before its motion. Because its motion is an ascent and descent. The female organs, that, Irigaray says, are "touching" before they are a thing. That can't be named as "things" without reduction. That are defined by their "relation".

It isn't that to change the weight and force of English will *necessarily* make women's speaking possible. But to move the force in any language, create a slippage, *even for a moment...* to decentre the "thing", unmask the relation...

What I brought back to poetry from my job was a stutter that replicated surfaces imperfectly, like the television screen with the vertical hold broken, no story possible, just the voices

heard again & again without image. Those dark voices. & I wrote, not into the book's heart, but out of fear, to make the image come back to me. Any image. My coat & shoes. My faint moving at the edge of the screen, blood in my head not moving but the room moving & the blood still... so that to move the force for a moment only held for that moment. (The word "held" a stillness, relational, not a motion...) (The word "moment" not a thing...) The preposition so relational it could not hold a value, & could hardly keep from vanishing.

I still believe in the relations & not the name. The symbol of relation. Hidden tensity of the verbs without tense. Because the past tense exists IN us speaking, or is not anywhere. We can speak of it separately because our language permits it. The future tense too. They do not exist outside our bodies! But in us as memory, & desire. Those relations.

& If we are to free our memories, our desires, we must refuse to restrain ourselves

Thrushes

To get back to that purity. The woman and the "I forget" of her
shoulders. My friend, voice, hand a stutter at the edge of. What is.
Real trees with birds in the branches, wet tamarack, the birds'
feathers glossed up & beaks singing. The throats birds have, oh soft
spotted brown

Oh name of the bird

Thrush

Do I have you beside me, me who is so small, the seeds I have
gnawed ache inside of me, do I have you beside me, bird. Take the
cup of wine away from me, so I won't fill it again. Take away the
telephone number of my friend I am hurting

Grief, now; the hand prevents me. The woman stands up on the
chair, so much have her shoulders forgotten, her legs gleam in the
light off the metal sheds, the tree, the soft throat smaller than my
hand, flit, spotted,
out of which, the warble

After awhile it becomes too easy, that surface you know so well. As if the animals could jump off the coins, their antlers burnished. Into the street, where you put *palm trees*. The line suffers from you. You don't want the ragged edge any more. You're wearing a black sweater with large buttons & your friends are smoking cigarettes in the cafe, waiting for you to get back so they can order. You're not in the toilet where you say you have gone, you are watching the smoke rise & holding the business card of the restaurant. You may be hungry. You pray that the fish who have come here have travelled a long distance.

Distance

After awhile the surface folds up into its mathematical planes. Because of physical solidity you can wear your sweater without it falling thru you. Grateful for this. You want to write only the gaps, between the eyelids of the letters. Transcribing the view has become impossible. We are what we paint & you have never painted. Only one picture, & that a long time ago, of the sea.

Sea

A woman in the restaurant is pouring a yellow liquid into the glass. Beer, cerveza, bier, bière, μπίρα. The palm trees & I'm not trying to buffalo you. It's the inside of kitchens where you want to go. The meat slicer, the steam cabinet, the steel deep of the sinks, the wire whisk, pierced and unpierced spoons they call female & male. "Hand me a female spoon", they say. You are wearing your white suit & a hairnet. The female imaginary exists, you are shure of it, & when you go you are taking the spoons.

Spoons

Your friends have ordered drinks & are sipping them. The line ends where it wants to. The surface is thirsty. A small fish laps at the ocean door. Its scales are chips of mica intermixed with carved wood. When you hold one to your mouth, you can whistle through it. The stars come on. Your friends have begun to talk literally in your absence. You whistle by touching the fish with your lips. Wherever you are, you hope you are smiling when you come to. It's hospitals make you nervous. The fish sings a popular song. The restaurant is full. In a few minutes, you will lose your reservations.

Reservations

A woman comes in wearing a coat & walks past you, brushing your sweater.

Sweater

You have watched your friends a long time. Already they have worn out the topic of literature & who is famous enough. They have ordered Italian food by demanding to know what it is, first, in English. A piccatina is a small piccata, the waiter says. There is a palm tree potted behind him. The edges were written by someone else. Each note on the page was a refusal, of the end of the line, a refusal of "the title", & a refusal of the "middle" of the poem. You will write again & give up your claim to the surface. The kitchen light is on in your own kitchen. The fish has come from very far away & brings with it the smell of ocean & a small door. You will get out of the ending by falling fully-clothed into the sea.

One of Canada's most eminent and respected poets and author of eighteen books of poetry, **ERÍN MOURE** is also a translator of poetry from French, Spanish, Galician, and Portuguese. Moure's work has received the Governor General's Literary Award, the Pat Lowther Memorial Award, two A. M. Klein Prizes, and has been a three-time finalist for the Griffin Poetry Prize, among others. Most recently, her poem/play *Kapusta* was shortlisted for the 2018 Kobzar Literary Award and her translation of Wilson Bueno's *Paraguayan Sea* was a finalist for a 2018 Best Translated Book Award in Poetry. Moure holds two honourary doctorates, from the University of Vigo in Galicia, Spain, and from Brandon University in Manitoba. She lives in Montreal.

LIST

The A List